microQuests

ultra-organized cell systems

Rebecca L. Johnson

illustrations by Jack Desrocher

diagrams by Jennifer E. Fairman, CMI

M Millbrook Press • Minneapolis

For ECW, who helps me avoid becoming *too* organized. —RLJ

Many of the photographs in this book are micrographs. Micrographs are photos taken through a microscope. Sometimes bright colors are added to micrographs to make cell parts easier to see. Other times, cells are stained with dye so cells and cell structures show up more clearly under a microscope.

As you read this book, look for the bold words in colored boxes. These words tell you about the photos and diagrams. You can also look for the lines that connect the photos and the text.

Millbrook Press
A division of Lerner Publishing Group, Inc.
241 First Avenue North
Minneapolis, MN 55401 U.S.A.

Website address: www.lernerbooks.com

Library of Congress Cataloging-in-Publication Data

Johnson, Rebecca L.
    Ultra-organized cell systems / by Rebecca L. Johnson ; illustrations by Jack Desrocher ; diagrams by Jennifer E. Fairman.
        p.   cm. — (Microquests)
    Includes bibliographical references and index.
    ISBN: 978–0–8225–7138–4 (lib. bdg. : alk. paper)
    1. Physiology—Juvenile literature. 2. Tissues—Juvenile literature. 3. Organs (Anatomy)—Juvenile literature. I. Desrocher, Jack, ill. II. Title.
QP37.J645 2008
612—dc22   2006036395

Manufactured in the United States of America
1 2 3 4 5 6 – DP – 13 12 11 10 09 08

table of contents

your organized body

You hear a knock at the door. Your mother stands in the doorway. Her eyes get big as she scans your bedroom.

Shirts and socks lie in heaps on the floor. Pants hang from open dresser drawers. Papers and books cover the desk. CDs and magazines are scattered across the bed.

"I've never seen such a mess!" your mother cries. "How can you *live* like this? How can you be *so* utterly disorganized?"

Does your room look like a tornado just hit it? Then maybe "disorganized" is a good description of your personal space. But you, yourself? That's a very different story. The truth is, you're far more organized than you—or your parents—might think.

Being organized is something all living things have in common. Living things are made from simple structures that combine to form more complex parts. That's true for every living thing on Earth. Including you.

The secret of your organized self lies deep within you. It all starts with your cells.

Cells are the basic units of life. They are like building blocks or Legos. Except something built of cells is alive.

A single cell is tiny. Hundreds of cells could fit inside the period at the end of this sentence. Your body contains trillions of cells.

But hang on. Cells are built of smaller parts too. They're made up of molecules. And molecules are made up of atoms. Atoms make up everything in the universe. Everything from stars and smoke to spaghetti and sea lions is made of atoms.

Atoms combine in different ways to form molecules. Molecules come in many shapes and sizes. But neither atoms nor molecules are alive. Cells are the smallest *living* things. Each one is made of millions of molecules.

To form cells, the right kinds of molecules must come together in just the right ways. Cells are the beginning of all living things. They're the starting point for your very organized body!

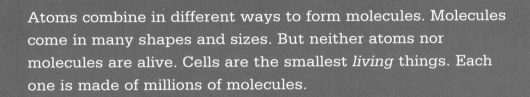

atoms

molecules

cells

cell basics

So how organized are cells? Be prepared to be impressed!

To get a good look at a cell, we need to use a microscope. Then we can see that a cell is packed with tiny structures. These are organelles. Each organelle has a specific job. The organelles work together to keep the cell alive and well.

Cells are like tiny factories. The organelles are the workers. They never rest. Organelles make and do whatever cells need to live and grow.

In any factory, someone has to be in charge. Inside a cell, the boss is a molecule. It's not just any molecule, though. It's a long, complex molecule called DNA. DNA is short for deoxyribonucleic acid.

As shown here, DNA looks like a twisted ladder. It contains the instructions for building a cell and controlling everything it does. But that's not all. In living things made of many cells (like you), DNA holds the instructions for making ALL the cells in an entire body. That's a big job. It's a much bigger job than building a skyscraper. Or even a space shuttle.

The cells in your body all have the same DNA. It came from your parents. Half your DNA came from your mother. The other half came from your father. Unless you have an identical twin, no one else has DNA exactly like yours.

DNA is in charge of everything at the cell factory. And that's a lot, as you can see:

The nucleus is the main office of the factory. DNA is inside the nucleus. The DNA sends instructions to other parts of the cell to keep things running smoothly.

Factories need power to run. So do cells. Mitochondria provide the power cells need for everything they do.

Microfilaments and microtubules form an almost invisible framework in the cell. Think of them as the beams and girders in a factory building.

Cytosol is a syrupy liquid—almost a gel. It surrounds all the organelles.

Lysosomes are little sacs filled with powerful chemicals. They're the cell's cleanup crew. They release their chemicals to break down old or damaged cell parts.

The cell membrane surrounds the entire cell. It's like a wall around the factory. But this wall has special "doors." These doors control what can enter and leave the cell.

Instructions from DNA go to ribosomes. The instructions tell the ribosomes to make protein molecules. Proteins are used to build most of the structures inside a cell.

Proteins move from the ribosomes to the endoplasmic reticulum, or ER. The ER is like a factory conveyor belt. As molecules move along inside the ER, small changes are made to them.

Finished proteins are packaged into vesicles. These little sacs form near the end of the ER. Vesicles are like factory messengers. They deliver things to other locations. Vesicles that leave the ER often head for the Golgi complex.

The Golgi complex is like a factory's mail room. It packages proteins and other molecules. Then it attaches chemical "labels" to them. The labels tell where the molecules are supposed to go.

Every one of your trillions of cells is busy all day and all night. But your cells don't look exactly like the one on the previous page. That cell is a "typical" cell. And there really is no such thing.

Real cells have different shapes and sizes. Some cells are long and thin. Some are round and plump. Others have wacky shapes. Some of your cells are packed with mitochondria. Others don't need very many.

In all, your body has about two hundred different kinds of cells. Why so many? You have a lot going on inside you. Many jobs need to be done. And different types of cells do different things.

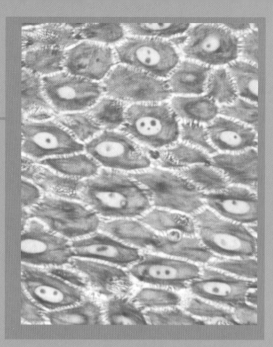

Take **skin cells**, for example. They cover the outside of your entire body. Under a microscope, you can see that skin cells are packed together with no space in between. You have about 300 million skin cells. They form a stretchy, waterproof, germproof covering for your body. Skin cells protect your insides from the outside world.

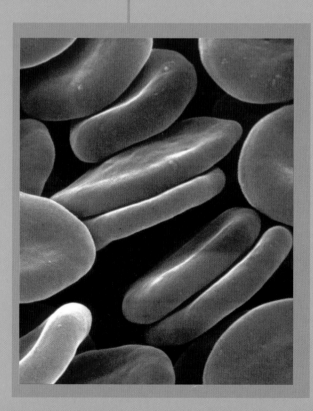

Your **red blood cells** are round and red. Their middles curve in, like someone pinched them really hard. Red blood cells are always moving. They carry important substances to all the cells in your body. You have about 25 billion of these little red cells cruising around inside you!

You also have **white blood cells**. Some are round. Others can change their shape. White blood cells find and destroy invaders, such as bacteria and viruses. These germs can make you sick.

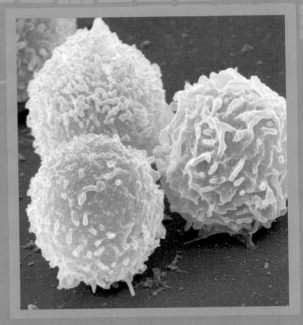

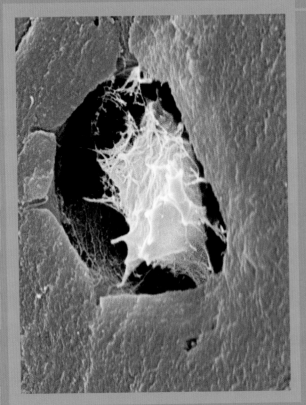

Bone cells are builders. They make—guess what?—your bones. Bone cells use matrix for building. They make matrix themselves. It contains lots of minerals. After it's made, matrix hardens around bone cells like concrete. That's what makes your bones so hard and strong.

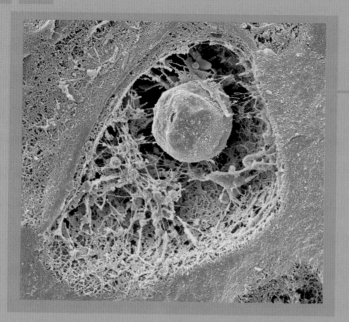

Like bone cells, **cartilage cells** are builders too. But they make cartilage, which is more like rubber than concrete. Where in your body can you find cartilage cells? Try the bendable parts of your ears and the rubbery tip of your nose.

As you might expect, **fat cells** are plump and rounded. Most of the space in a fat cell is filled with liquid fat. There may be so much fat in a cell that it squeezes the nucleus and other organelles off to the sides!

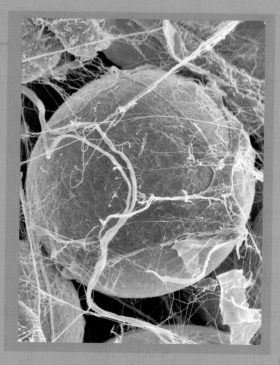

Nerve cells might win the award for most sensitive cells. They're designed for sending and receiving messages—at split-second speeds. Some nerve cells have really long "tails."

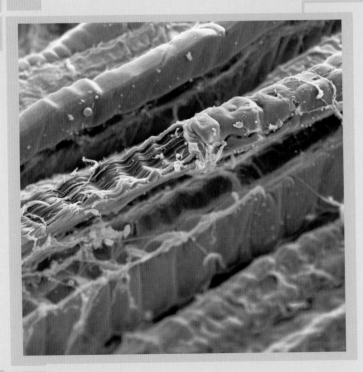

Muscle cells are usually long and lean. What's their special skill? Muscle cells can move. They have proteins that contract, or shorten. Muscle cells pull and move body parts.

Muscle cells, nerve cells, and bone cells are just a few of the many kinds of cells in your body. Each one is organized. Each one is skilled at doing its job.

But by themselves, cells can't build and maintain the entire YOU. That's too much work for individuals. So cells organize themselves into teams. These talented teams of hard working cells are called tissues. And if you thought cells were organized, wait until you see what tissue teams can do!

chapter 3
a look at tissues

Tissues are groups of similar cells that do the same job.

To belong to a tissue team, a cell needs certain skills. It needs to be able to recognize other tissue cells. And it must be able to communicate with them. Cells that communicate with one another can work together.

Cells in a tissue recognize one another by certain types of molecules on their cell membranes. These molecules are like team colors or logos. They help cells know who's who.

Tissue cells also have to physically stick together. They have places on their cell membranes that link to other cells. By being connected in this way, many cells can act as one.

You have many tissues in your body. These tissues belong to four main groups: epithelial, connective, nervous, and muscle tissue.

Epithelial tissue covers the outside and lines the inside of most of your body parts. Cells in epithelial tissue are tightly joined to one another. Together they form tough, stretchy sheets. Some types of 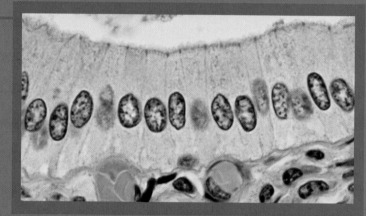 epithelial tissue are made of a single sheet of cells. Others are built from several sheets, stacked in layers. Epithelial tissue protects the body. It guards against germs. It also protects other body parts from getting hurt.

Where do you find this tissue? Run your tongue across the roof of your mouth. The slippery surface up there is epithelial tissue. Your stomach is lined with a similar kind. So are your intestines. Epithelial tissue even covers your eyeballs and the inside of your nose.

Your **skin** is your most
obvious epithelial
tissue. Sheets of
epithelial cells form
skin's outer layer.

Cells at the skin's
surface are packed
with keratin. That's a
protein that makes the
cells strong and
waterproof. These
cells are tough. But
they don't live very
long. Dead epithelial
cells cover your skin.
Scratch your skin and
hundreds, even
thousands, flake off.

New epithelial cells are always forming beneath the skin's
surface. These cells move up to replace dead cells. In fact, all
your skin's epithelial cells are replaced every seventy-five days!

Inside and out, your body has a lot of epithelial tissue. But you have even more connective tissue. Connective tissue is good for packing and padding. It holds things together and connects them.

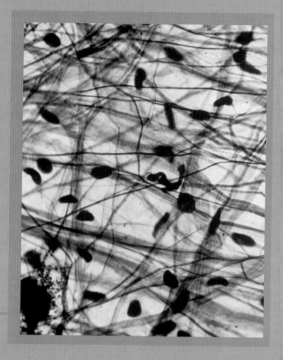

Connective tissue comes in different forms. Beneath the epithelial tissue in your skin, you have a layer of **loose connective tissue**. The name says it all. It's a loose collection of cells, fibers, and fluid. This tissue connects the outside of your skin to tissues farther in.

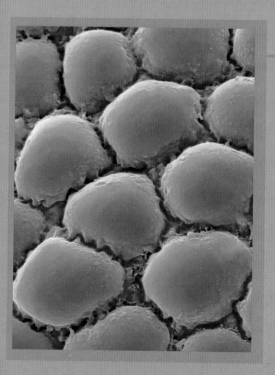

Fat tissue is a special type of loose connective tissue. It's mostly made up of (you guessed it!) fat cells. Patches of fat tissue are your body's pillows. They cushion you from bumps and falls. Fat tissue traps heat inside your body. The heat helps keep you warm. Fat tissue also helps out if you don't have enough food. If you don't get enough to eat, your body will start using fat to get the energy it needs.

Dense connective tissue contains lots of strong, stretchy fibers. In some cases, the fibers go every which way. In others, they are organized into rows. **Tendons** are made of dense connective tissue. They have fibers that all run in the same direction. Like giant rubber bands, tendons connect muscles to bones.

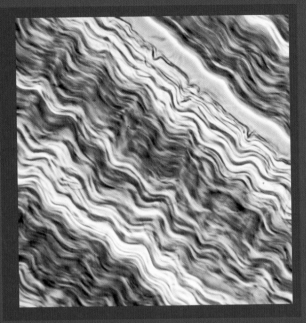

And speaking of bones, **bone** is a connective tissue too. Bone is made up of bone cells and fibers, plus the hard matrix. Bone cells live in tiny pockets of matrix. They're arranged in circles around openings in bone tissue.

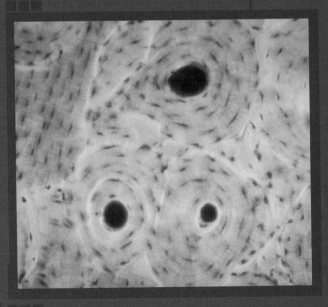

Wherever you find bone, you'll usually find **cartilage** close by. Cartilage is a connective tissue. It's made of cartilage cells and fibers, plus a rubbery matrix that the cartilage cells make. Cartilage isn't as strong as bone. But it can bend (up to a point) without breaking. Bone and cartilage tissues build a strong frame for your body.

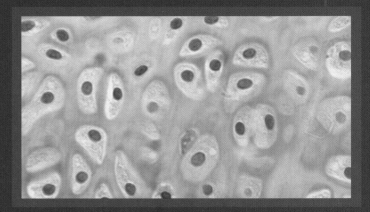

Blood is also a connective tissue—a liquid one. Blood contains white blood cells, red blood cells, and platelets. Platelets are tiny cell pieces. All your blood cells float in a watery liquid called plasma.

Blood has two main jobs. It brings oxygen (a gas) and nutrients (chemicals from food) to cells. And it carries away their wastes. In this way, blood connects all the parts of your body.

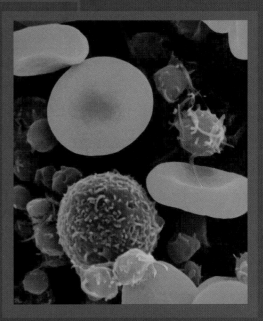

Nervous tissue is the third major kind of tissue. Nervous tissue has lots of nerve cells. But it has even more smaller cells. They're called supporting cells. They take care of the nerve cells in nervous tissue.

Supporting cells hold nerve cells in place. They help protect them. And supporting cells make sure that nerve cells can do what *they* do best: send and receive messages.

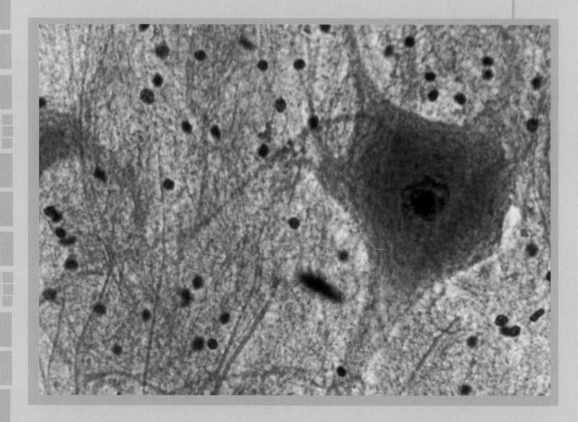

Muscle tissue is tissue type number four. You can probably guess that it has lots of muscle cells. Remember that muscle cells can contract. In muscle tissue, many muscle cells all contract at the same time. While a single cell can pull just a little, a million cells contracting together can pull a lot!

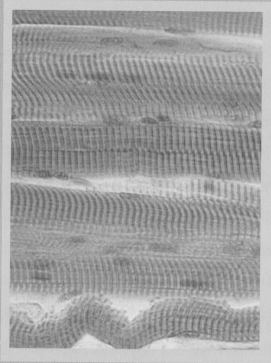

Not all the muscle tissue in your body is the same. **Skeletal muscle tissue** is made of long, sturdy muscle cells. They contract very quickly. This tissue has enough power to move whole body parts. But if it contracts too many times, it gets tired.

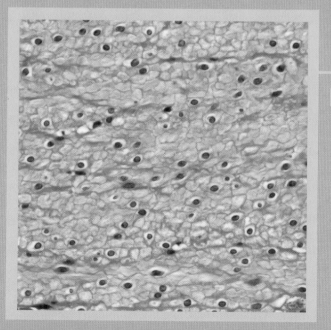

Smooth muscle tissue is formed from shorter, thinner muscle cells. This tissue contracts more slowly. It almost never gets tired. Smooth muscle helps move things through your body, like food through your stomach.

Heart muscle tissue is found only in your heart. Heart muscle cells are short and branched. They're tightly connected. The close connections help heart muscle cells work *really* well together.

Heart muscle tissue is the superstar of the muscle tissue world. It never gets tired of contracting. And during your entire lifetime, it will never stop.

Day after day, groups of heart muscle cells contract and relax with perfect timing. This tissue contracts with just the right amount of force to pump just the right amount of blood through your heart.

Your heart, of course, is made of more than just heart muscle tissue. You'll also find epithelial tissue, connective tissue, and nervous tissue there. Your heart is a combination of different kinds of tissues, all working together.

The four main tissues in your body are "organ-ized" to form organs. Tissue teams work together in organs to keep your body going.

a glimpse at organs

Your body's organs are made from groups of tissues. (A group means at least two different kinds of tissues.) The tissues in an organ cooperate. Together they carry out tough jobs.

A heart is just one of your organs. You also have a brain. A liver. A spleen and a stomach. Kidneys and lungs. Eyes and ears. The list goes on and on.

Each organ is made up of a unique group of tissues. No two organs are alike. Except, of course, organ pairs, such as eyes and lungs! Let's take a closer look at some of your organs. See how many familiar tissues and cells you can spot.

Your heart is a living pump. It's about the size of your fist. Every day, this organ moves all your blood around your body at least one thousand times!

A **human heart** has four chambers, or sections. Every time the heart beats, these chambers contract, or squeeze. The squeezing forces blood out of the heart and into blood vessels. (More about those in a moment.)

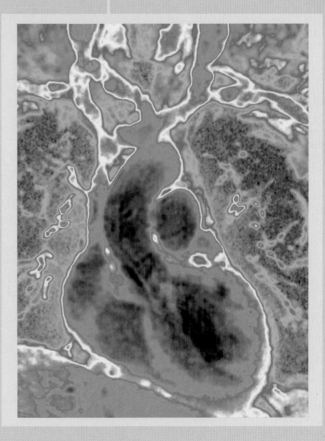

Heart muscle tissue does the squeezing. Epithelial tissue lines the heart's chambers. Tough, stretchy bits of connective tissue form little doors between the chambers. Nervous tissue reaches deep into the heart's muscle tissue. It sends messages to the muscle cells, telling them when and how hard to contract.

The heart pumps blood through blood vessels. Blood vessels are organs too. You have miles and miles of them. Some are big and sturdy. Others are tiny. They reach into every part of your body.

This small blood vessel carries blood away from the heart. Red blood cells are packed inside. The vessel is round, like a tube. Its walls are formed from several tissues. Epithelial tissue lines the inside. Next is a bit of stretchy connective tissue and a narrow ring of smooth muscle tissue. The muscle tissue contracts to push blood along.

Your heart sits in between two other large organs—your lungs. Each lung is made up of 300 million tiny **air sacs**. The sacs connect to tiny tubes. These tubes join to form larger tubes. As you breathe, air moves through the tubes and in and out of the sacs.

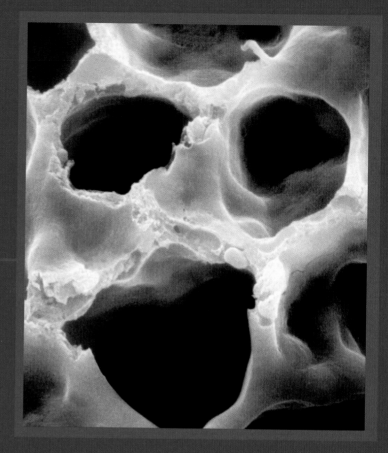

The walls of the air sacs are very thin. A single layer of epithelial cells lines both sides. In between are connective tissue, a bit of smooth muscle, and the smallest of blood vessels. That's it!

When you breathe in, a gas called oxygen enters your lungs. This gas passes through the thin air sac walls and into the blood vessels in the lungs. There, red blood cells grab the oxygen and carry it to your body's other cells. When the body cells accept the oxygen, they release another gas into the blood. This gas is carbon dioxide. Blood carries carbon dioxide back to the lungs. When you breathe out, that gas leaves your body.

Your stomach breaks down the food you eat. It squeezes and churns to mash food into tiny pieces. It also adds chemicals that turn solid food into a liquid. It's all part of digestion.

Epithelial tissue lines the inside of the stomach. That lining is packed with cells. Some make digestive chemicals, which break down food. Others produce mucus. That's a thick, slimy goo. It prevents the digestive juice from breaking down your stomach too!

Beneath the stomach lining are connective tissue, nervous tissue, and small blood vessels. The stomach also has two layers of smooth muscle tissue. When these muscles contract, the stomach twists and turns.

epithelial tissue

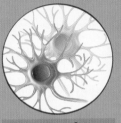
nervous tissue

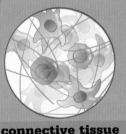
connective tissue

blood vessels

smooth muscle tissue

Bones are organs too. You have 206 of them. They come in many shapes and sizes. But they all have the same basic structure.

Living bones are covered with a thin layer of tough connective tissue. They may have cartilage tissue on some parts of their surface. Beneath these tissues lies solid bone tissue. It is organized into a pattern of ringlike shapes. Small blood vessels run through the holes in the center of each ring. Bones also have nervous tissue, which is why broken bones hurt!

The center of most bones isn't solid. It's a maze of small bony bridges that are separated by spaces. The spaces are filled with a soft tissue called bone marrow. Many of your blood cells are formed in the marrow.

cartilage

connective tissue

solid bone tissue

blood vessels and nerves

bone marrow

Your brain weighs about 2 to 3 pounds (0.9 to 1.4 kilograms). That's about the same weight as a cauliflower. The brain is the body's control center. It's in charge of everything you think, say, and do.

The brain is made of lots of nervous tissue. It's home to more than 100 billion nerve cells! You also have blood vessels in your brain. And several layers of connective tissue wrap around the outside of the **brain**.

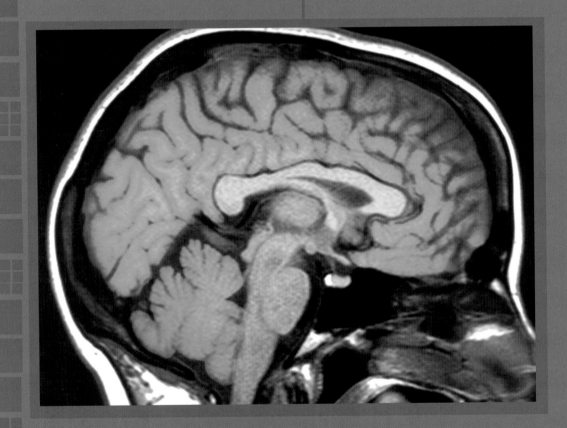

Your largest organ is your skin. Skin protects you from sun, dirt, and germs. It helps keep you warm and dry. It also locks water inside your body so your other cells, tissues, and organs don't dry out.

Skin has three layers. You've already met the top one. It's epithelial tissue. The middle layer is connective tissue. It's packed with blood vessels and nerve cells. Some nerve cells sense pressure. Others pick up heat, cold, or pain. The middle layer of skin has tiny hairs and glands too. Glands are formed from special epithelial cells. Those in your skin make sweat or oil. Skin's bottom layer is also connective tissue. It's plumped up with fat cells for good padding.

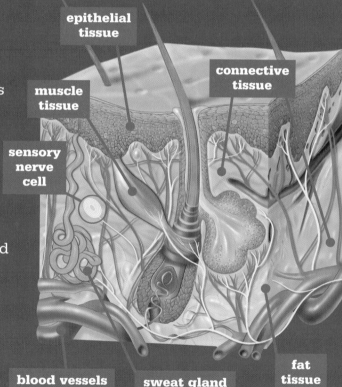

epithelial tissue

connective tissue

muscle tissue

sensory nerve cell

blood vessels

sweat gland

fat tissue

It's hard to imagine anything more organized than skin. Or a brain or a heart or lungs. But organs are not the final step. Can you guess what's next?

chapter 5

a peek at organ systems

If cells form tissues and tissues form organs, can organs work together too? They sure can! Organs that work together to do a job form an organ system. You have twelve organ systems in your organized body.

Your **circulatory system** is your heart, blood vessels, and all your blood. It moves oxygen, nutrients, and other substances through your body.

The **respiratory system** brings oxygen to your blood. (Your cells can't live without oxygen.) It also gets rid of the carbon dioxide that cells produce. Your lungs, nose, mouth, and trachea are all part of the respiratory team.

nose

mouth

trachea

lungs

heart

blood vessels

Your **integumentary system** includes your skin, hair, and nails. These organs keep you warm when it's cold and cool when it's hot. They work together to protect against damage or invasion by germs.

For females, reproductive organs include the ovaries and uterus. For males, reproductive organs include the testes and several ducts and glands. The main job of the **reproductive system** is to make new humans!

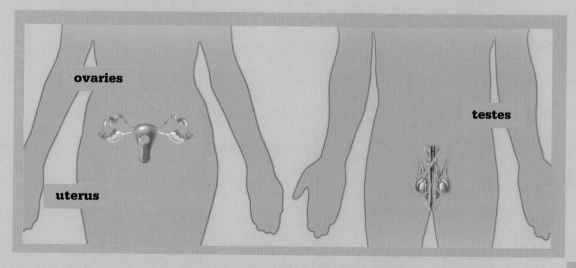

ovaries

testes

uterus

Your **skeletal system** includes your bones, cartilage, tendons, and ligaments. (Ligaments are similar to tendons. They connect bones to other bones.) Your skeletal system holds you up. It supports all your other body systems and structures. Parts of the system, such as your skull and your rib cage, protect the brain, heart, lungs, and other organs.

bone

cartilage

muscles

Muscles make up the **muscular system**. Without this system, you couldn't move. Because of it, you can ride a bike, dance, brush your teeth, and much, much more. Muscles also take care of things you hardly ever think about. This includes breathing, blinking, and swallowing.

ligament

tendon

The **digestive system** breaks down food into nutrients. Your cells need nutrients to live and grow. This system includes your mouth, esophagus, stomach, and intestines. Organs such as your liver also help with digestion.

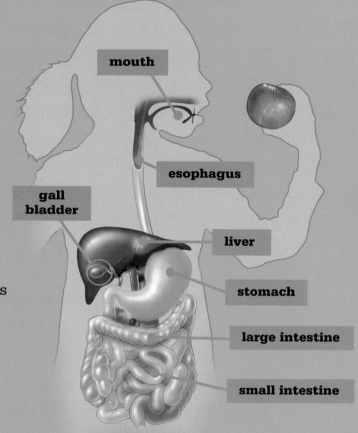

mouth

esophagus

gall bladder

liver

stomach

large intestine

small intestine

kidneys

The **excretory system** is how your body gets rid of liquid waste. It includes your kidneys, bladder, and a lot of tubes. Together these organs filter out wastes and extra water from your blood.

bladder

Your **nervous system** handles the body's communication. Thanks to this system, information—in the form of nerve impulses—zips around your body. Nerve impulses are fast-moving messages. Your brain, spinal cord, and nerves handle these messages. The nervous system controls how you move and behave. It also helps your other systems do their jobs.

brain

spinal cord

nerves

pituitary gland

thyroid gland

adrenal glands

Your **endocrine system** sends messages too. But it uses chemicals called hormones to do it. Glands such as the pituitary, thyroid, and adrenal glands make up this system. It works closely with the nervous system. This system directs many basic body processes, such as how much and how fast you grow.

The **lymphatic system** has many vessels that reach deep into all your tissues. These vessels pick up fluid produced by cells and return it to your blood. Tiny swellings called lymph nodes are scattered along lymph vessels. They work to catch germs, such as bacteria and viruses, that might be in your body fluids. The lymphatic system makes some of your white blood cells. Organs in this system include your tonsils, thymus, and spleen.

The **immune system** works closely with the lymphatic system. It's made up of an army of cells. Some of these cells are made in organs of the lymphatic system. Others form in bone marrow. Immune system cells are always on duty. They knock out and destroy bacteria, viruses, and other invaders.

tonsils

thymus

lymph node

spleen

lymph vessel

organized organisms

Congratulations! You've followed a long path to learn how organized you really are. The journey has taken you from cells to tissues to organs to systems. At last, we've come to the final step: the whole organism. In your case, that's you!

An organism is the body of an entire living thing. It's the sum of all its parts. All organisms have a few things in common. For example, they all need energy. They all reproduce. And of course, don't forget that all organisms are made of cells.

We are all made of cells!

Some organisms are just one single cell. That's the case with bacteria, **amoebas**, and other microscopic life-forms. Single-celled organisms don't have tissues and organs. Their cell *is* their body. It's really all they need.

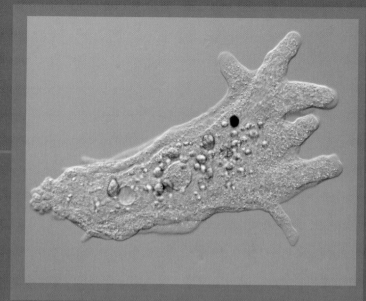

Multicellular organisms have bodies built from many cells. You belong to this group. So do catfish, honeybees, and toadstools. And palm trees, pandas, snails, and whales. So do countless other living things.

Whether they have millions or billions or trillions of cells, most multicellular organisms have something important in common with you. If you study them closely, you'll discover that they have systems made up of organs . . . and organs made up of tissues . . . and tissues made up of cells, which are built from molecules and atoms.

That's right! Literally millions of living things are organized just . . . like . . . you!

glossary

atoms: tiny structures that make up everything in the universe

cartilage: a rubbery type of connective tissue formed by cartilage cells

cell: the smallest unit of life. Cells are building blocks of living things.

cell membrane: the covering that surrounds a cell and controls what leaves and enters it

connective tissue: a type of tissue that connects other tissues and forms packing and filling material in the body

contract: to pull together or shorten

cytosol: the gel that fills a cell and surrounds the cell's organelles

digestion: the process of breaking down food into substances that cells can use

deoxyribonucleic acid (DNA): the material in cells that carries the complete set of instructions for building an organism

endocrine (EHN-doh-krin) system: organ system that sends chemical messages to body parts

endoplasmic reticulum (ER): an organelle in cells that processes newly made proteins

epithelial (eh-puh-THEE-lee-uhl) tissue: a type of tissue that covers surfaces and lines body cavities

gland: a group of cells that makes and releases chemicals and other substances the body needs

Golgi complex: an organelle in cells that processes and packages proteins

hormone: a chemical released in the body (often by a gland) that controls how other cells, tissues, or organs function

integumentary (in-teg-yoo-MEN-tuh-ree) system: organ system that includes skin, hair, and nails

keratin: a protein that makes skin cells tough and waterproof

lysosome: an organelle in cells that helps break down worn-out parts of a cell

matrix: a substance released by cells that forms their immediate surroundings; it can be hard, rubbery, or liquid

microfilament: a threadlike structure that helps cells move

microtubule: a tubelike structure that provides support in a cell and moves organelles from place to place

mitochondria: organelles in cells that provide the power that cells need for everything they do

molecule: a group of atoms held tightly together

mucus: a slimy substance produced by some epithelial tissue cells

multicellular: having more than one cell

nucleus: an organelle that contains a cell's DNA

nutrients: the broken-down products of digestion that cells need to live and grow

organ: a body structure made up of different tissues that work together

organelle: a small structure that does a specific job inside a cell

organism: an entire living thing

plasma: the liquid part of blood

platelets: tiny cell pieces in blood

proteins: the chemical building blocks of cells

reproductive system: the organ system that makes new organisms with cells from existing organisms

ribosome: a cell organelle that makes proteins, using instructions from DNA

supporting cells: types of cells that help nerve cells in nervous tissue

system: a group of organs that work together to do a job in a body

tissue: a group of similar cells that work together

vesicle: a small sac containing substances inside a cell

read more about cells, tissues, organs, and systems

Books

Barter, James. *Organ Transplants*. Farmington Hills, MI: Lucent Books, 2006.

Johnson, Rebecca L. *The Digestive System*. Minneapolis: Lerner Publications Company, 2005.

———. *The Muscular System*. Minneapolis: Lerner Publications Company, 2005.

Showers, Paul. *A Drop of Blood*. New York: HarperCollins, 2004.

Websites

All Systems Go
http://www.sciencenetlinks.com/interactives/systems.html
Put Arnold's organ systems inside his body. To succeed, you'll need to know which organs belong to which organ system.

BBC—Science & Nature—Human Body & Mind—Interactive Body
http://www.bbc.co.uk/science/humanbody/body/index_interactivebody.shtml
This site has games to teach you about the organs, the muscular system, the skeletal system, the nervous system, and the senses.

Cell Models: An Interactive Animation
http://www.cellsalive.com/cells/cell_model.htm
Click on organelles to find out what they look like and what they do.

Human Anatomy Online
http://www.innerbody.com/htm/body.html
This website explores body systems, organs, tissues, and cells.

My Body
http://kidshealth.org/kid/body/mybody_noSW.html
Learn more about your organs and body systems. This website includes lots of fun diagrams.

index

about the author

Rebecca L. Johnson is the author of many award-winning science books for children. Her previous books include the Biomes of North America series, *The Digestive System, The Muscular System, Genetics,* and *Plate Tectonics.* Ms. Johnson lives in Sioux Falls, South Dakota.

photo acknowledgments

The images in this book are used with the permission of: © Comstock Images, p. 9; © Biophoto Associates/Photo Researchers, Inc., p. 13 (top); © Dr. David M. Phillips/Visuals Unlimited, pp. 13 (bottom), 22 (bottom); © SPL/Photo Researchers, Inc., p. 14 (both); © Steve Gschmeissner/Photo Researchers, Inc., p. 15 (both); © David McCarthy/Photo Researchers, Inc., p. 16 (top); © Eye of Science/Photo Researchers, Inc., p. 16 (bottom); © Ed Reschke/Peter Arnold, Inc., p. 19; © Dennis Kunkel Microscopy, Inc., pp. 20, 21 (bottom), 23 (bottom), 26, 30; © Dr. John D. Cunningham/Visuals Unlimited, pp. 21 (top), 25 (top); © Biology Media/Photo Researchers, Inc., p. 22 (top); © Chuck Brown/Photo Researchers, Inc., p. 23 (top); © Henry Robison/Visuals Unlimited, p. 24; © Dr. G. W. Willis/Visuals Unlimited, p. 25 (bottom); © BSIP/Photo Researchers, Inc., p. 29; © Dr. John Sasner/UNH/Visuals Unlimited, p. 31; © Edward Kinsman/Photo Researchers, Inc., p. 34; © Sam Lund/Independent Picture Service, p. 37; © Wim van Egmond/Visuals Unlimited, p. 43.

Front Cover: © Dennis Kunkel Microscopy, Inc. (background), © Lerner Publishing Group, Inc. (illustration)